THE COLDPLAY COLLECTION

PARACHUTES:
Don't Panic 5
Shiver 8
Spies 15
Sparks 22
Yellow 26
Trouble 32
Parachutes 37
High Speed 39
We Never Change 43
Everything's Not Lost 49
Life Is For Living 58

A RUSH OF BLOOD TO THE HEAD:
Politik 65
In My Place 70
God Put A Smile Upon Your Face 74
The Scientist 81
Clocks 86
Daylight 92
Green Eyes 99
Warning Sign 105
A Whisper 112
A Rush Of Blood To The Head 117
Amsterdam 125

X&Y:
Square One 135
What If 144
White Shadows 149
Fix You 156
Talk 162
X&Y 170
Speed Of Sound 176
A Message 182
Low 189
The Hardest Part 196
Swallowed In The Sea 203
Twisted Logic 210
Til Kingdom Come 216

VIVA LA VIDA OR DEATH AND ALL HIS FRIENDS:
Life In Technicolor 226
Cemeteries Of London 230
Lost! 235
42 239
Lovers In Japan 245
Reign Of Love 251
Yes 255
Chinese Sleep Chant 261
Viva La Vida 266
Violet Hill 272
Strawberry Swing 276
Death And All His Friends 281
The Escapist 286

WISE PUBLICATIONS
part of The Music Sales Group
London / New York / Paris / Sydney / Copenhagen / Berlin / Madrid / Tokyo

Published by
Wise Publications
14-15 Berners Street, London
W1T 3LJ, UK.

Exclusive distributors:
Music Sales Limited
Distribution Centre, Newmarket Road,
Bury St Edmunds, Suffolk,
IP33 3YB, UK.

Music Sales Pty Limited
20 Resolution Drive, Caringbah,
NSW 2229, Australia.

Order No. AM997040
ISBN 978-1-84938-018-8

This book © Copyright 2009 Wise Publications,
a division of Music Sales Limited.

Unauthorised reproduction of any part
of this publication by any means including
photocopying is an infringement of copyright.

Music arranged by Derek Jones and Jack Long.
Music processed by Paul Ewers Music Design.

A Rush Of Blood To The Head
Cover artwork courtesy of Blue Source.

X&Y
Original CD design by Tappin Gofton.
Photography by Kevin Westenberg, Tom Sheehan and Coldplay.

Viva La Vida
Cover painting by Eugéne Delacroix.
Original CD design by Tappin Gofton.
Photography by Dan Green and Guy Berryman.

Printed in the EU.

THE COLDPLAY COLLECTION

PARACHUTES

Your Guarantee of Quality:

As publishers, we strive to produce every book
to the highest commercial standards.

The music has been freshly engraved to make
playing from it a real pleasure. Particular care has been given
to specifying acid-free, neutral-sized paper made from pulps
which have not been elemental chlorine bleached.

This pulp is from farmed sustainable forests and
was produced with special regard for the environment.

Throughout, the printing and binding have been
planned to ensure a sturdy, attractive publication
which should give years of enjoyment.

If your copy fails to meet our high standards,
please inform us and we will gladly replace it.

www.musicsales.com

Don't Panic

Words & Music by Guy Berryman, Chris Martin, Jon Buckland & Will Champion

© Copyright 1999 Universal Music Publishing MGB Limited.
All Rights in Germany Administered by Musik Edition Discoton GmbH (A Division of Universal Music Publishing Group).
All Rights Reserved. International Copyright Secured.

Shiver

Words & Music by Guy Berryman, Chris Martin, Jon Buckland & Will Champion

Verse 2:
So you know how much I need you,
But you never even see me do you?
And is this my final chance of getting you?

But on and on, from the moment I wake *etc.*

Spies

Words & Music by Guy Berryman, Chris Martin, Jon Buckland & Will Champion

18

Verse 2:
I awake to see that no-one is free
We're all fugitives
Look at the way we live
Down here I cannot sleep from fear, no
I said "which way do I turn?"
Oh, I forget ev'rything I learn.

And the spies come out of the water *etc.*

Verse 2:
My heart is yours
It's you that I hold on to
That's what I do.
And I know I was wrong
But I won't let you down
Oh, yeah I will, yeah I will
Yes I will.

I said I
I cry I.

Yellow

Words & Music by Guy Berryman, Chris Martin, Jon Buckland & Will Champion

Verse 2:
I swam across, I jumped across for you.
Oh, what a thing to do,
'Cause you were all yellow.

I drew a line, I drew a line for you.
Oh, what a thing to do,
And it was all yellow.

Your skin, oh yeah, your skin and bones
Turn into something beautiful.
And you know, for you I'd bleed myself dry,
For you I'd bleed myself dry.

Trouble

Words & Music by Guy Berryman, Chris Martin, Jon Buckland & Will Champion

High Speed

Words & Music by Guy Berryman, Jon Buckland, Will Champion & Chris Martin

Everything's Not Lost

Words & Music by Guy Berryman, Chris Martin, Jon Buckland & Will Champion

1. And when I count-ed up my de-mons

saw there was one for ev-'ry day.

But with the good ones on my shoul-ders

© Copyright 2000 Universal Music Publishing MGB Limited.
All Rights in Germany Administered by Musik Edition Discoton GmbH (A Division of Universal Music Publishing Group).
All Rights Reserved. International Copyright Secured.

Life Is For Living

Words & Music by Guy Berryman, Jon Buckland, Will Champion & Chris Martin

THE COLDPLAY COLLECTION

A RUSH OF BLOOD TO THE HEAD

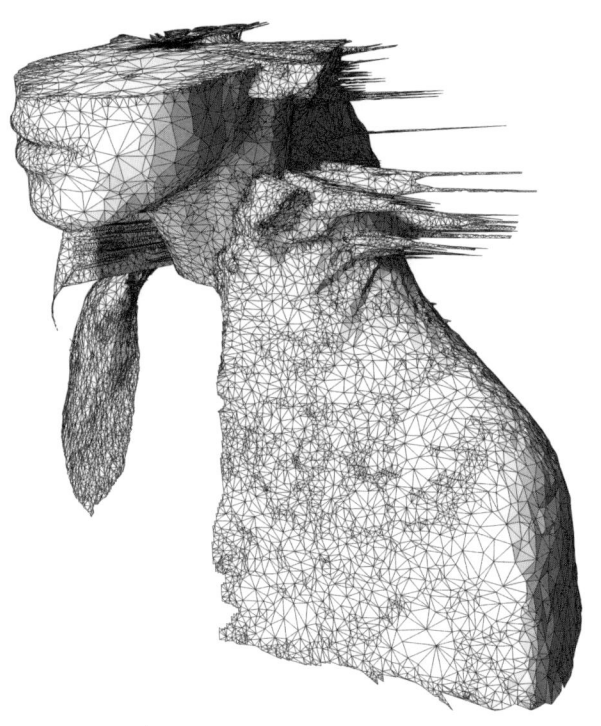

Politik

Words & Music by Guy Berryman, Chris Martin, Jon Buckland & Will Champion

© Copyright 2002 Universal Music Publishing MGB Limited.
All Rights in Germany Administered by Musik Edition Discoton GmbH (A Division of Universal Music Publishing Group).
All Rights Reserved. International Copyright Secured.

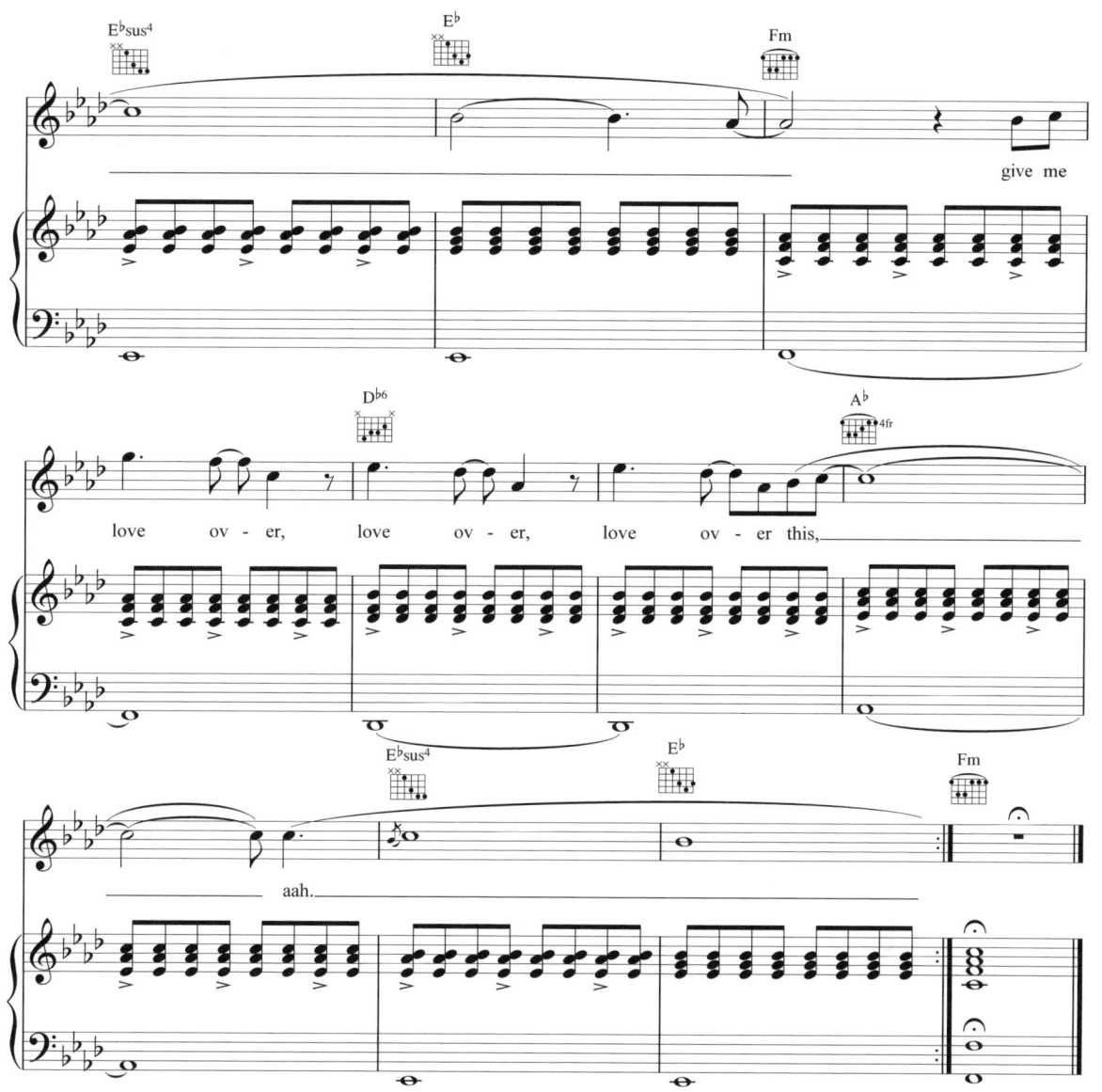

Verse 2:
Give me one, 'cause one is best
In confusion confidence
Give me peace of mind and trust
Don't forget the rest of us.
Give me strength, reserve, control
Give me heart and give me soul
Wounds that heal, and cracks that fix
Tell me your own politik.

And open up your eyes *etc.*

In My Place

Words & Music by Guy Berryman, Chris Martin, Jon Buckland & Will Champion

Verse 2:
I was scared, I was scared,
Tired and under-prepared,
But I'll wait for it.
And if you go, if you go
And leave me down here on my own,
Then I'll wait for you, yeah.

Yeah, how long must you wait *etc.*

God Put A Smile Upon Your Face

Words & Music by Guy Berryman, Chris Martin, Jon Buckland & Will Champion

© Copyright 2002 Universal Music Publishing MGB Limited.
All Rights in Germany Administered by Musik Edition Discoton GmbH (A Division of Universal Music Publishing Group).
All Rights Reserved. International Copyright Secured.

Verse 2:
Where do we go to draw the line?
I've got to say I wasted all your time honey, honey.
Where do I go to fall from grace?
God put a smile upon your face, yeah.

Verse 3:
Where do we go? Nobody knows.
Don't ever say you're on your way down, when
God gave you style and gave you grace
And put a smile upon your face.

Now, when you work it out *etc.*

Clocks

Words & Music by Guy Berryman, Chris Martin, Jon Buckland & Will Champion

Daylight

Words & Music by Guy Berryman, Jon Buckland, Will Champion & Chris Martin

Verse 2:
On a hilltop
On a sky-rise
Like a first-born child
On the full tilt
And in full flight
Defeat darkness
Breaking daylight.

Ooh and the sun will shine *etc.*

Green Eyes

Words & Music by Guy Berryman, Jon Buckland, Will Champion & Chris Martin

Verse 2:
Honey, you are the sea
Upon which I float
And I came here to talk
I think you should know
That Green Eyes
You're the one that I wanted to find
And anyone who tried to deny you
Must be out of their mind.

Because I came here with a load *etc.*

Warning Sign

Words & Music by Guy Berryman, Jon Buckland, Will Champion & Chris Martin

Verse 2:
A warning sign
You came back to haunt me
And I realised that you were an island
And I passed you by
When you were an island to discover.

Come on in
I've got to tell you what a state I'm in
I've got to tell you in my loudest tones
That I started looking for a warning sign.

When the truth is I miss you *etc*.

A Whisper

Words & Music by Guy Berryman, Chris Martin, Jon Buckland & Will Champion

A Rush Of Blood To The Head

Words & Music by Guy Berryman, Chris Martin, Jon Buckland & Will Champion

© Copyright 2002 Universal Music Publishing MGB Limited.
All Rights in Germany Administered by Musik Edition Discoton GmbH (A Division of Universal Music Publishing Group).
All Rights Reserved. International Copyright Secured.

Amsterdam

Words & Music by Guy Berryman, Chris Martin, Jon Buckland & Will Champion

Verse 3:
Come on, oh, my star is fading
And I see no chance of release
And I know I'm dead on the surface
But I am screaming underneath.

And time is on your side *etc.*

THE COLDPLAY COLLECTION

X&Y

What If

Words & Music by Guy Berryman, Chris Martin, Jon Buckland & Will Champion

© Copyright 2005 Universal Music Publishing MGB Limited.
All Rights in Germany Administered by Musik Edition Discoton GmbH (A Division of Universal Music Publishing Group).
All Rights Reserved. International Copyright Secured.

White Shadows

Words & Music by Guy Berryman, Chris Martin, Jon Buckland & Will Champion

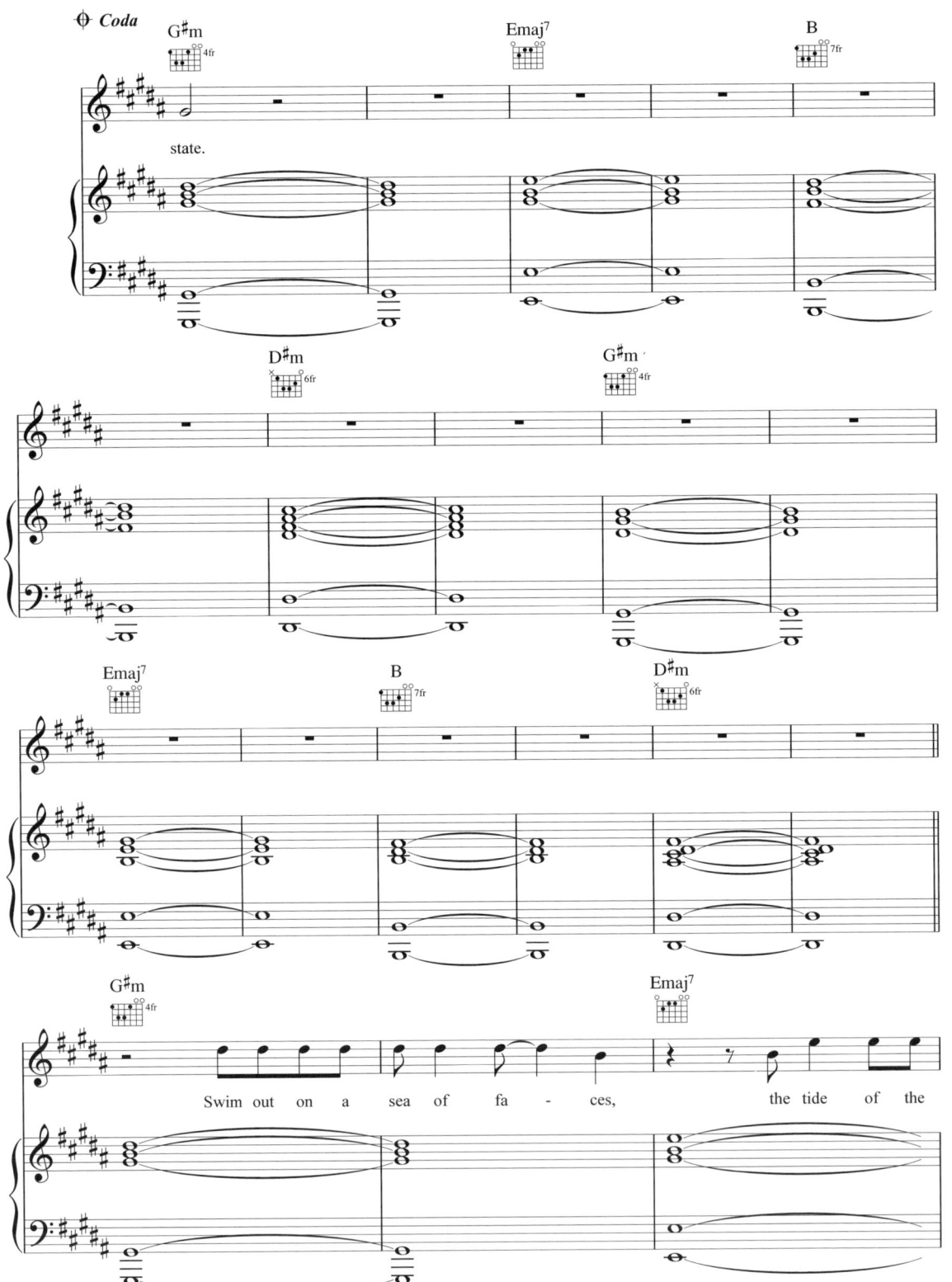

Fix You

Words & Music by Guy Berryman, Chris Martin, Jon Buckland & Will Champion

Talk

Words & Music by Guy Berryman, Chris Martin, Karl Bartos, Jon Buckland, Will Champion,
Emil Schult & Ralf Hütter

© Copyright 2005 Universal Music Publishing MGB Limited (50%)
(administered in Germany by Musik Edition Discoton GmbH)/Sony/ATV Music Publishing (UK) Limited (37.5%)/
Warner/Chappell Music Limited (12.5%).
All Rights Reserved. International Copyright Secured.

X&Y

Words & Music by Guy Berryman, Chris Martin, Jon Buckland & Will Champion

♩ = 76

Try-ing hard to speak and fight-ing with my weak hand, dri-ven to dis-trac-tion, it's all part of the plan. When some-thing is bro-ken and you try to fix it, try-ing to re-pair it a-ny way you can.

© Copyright 2005 Universal Music Publishing MGB Limited.
All Rights in Germany Administered by Musik Edition Discoton GmbH (A Division of Universal Music Publishing Group).
All Rights Reserved. International Copyright Secured.

Speed Of Sound

Words & Music by Guy Berryman, Chris Martin, Jon Buckland & Will Champion

Low

Words & Music by Guy Berryman, Chris Martin, Jon Buckland & Will Champion

The Hardest Part

Words & Music by Guy Berryman, Chris Martin, Jon Buckland & Will Champion

Swallowed In The Sea

Words & Music by Guy Berryman, Chris Martin, Jon Buckland & Will Champion

© Copyright 2005 Universal Music Publishing MGB Limited.
All Rights in Germany Administered by Musik Edition Discoton GmbH (A Division of Universal Music Publishing Group).
All Rights Reserved. International Copyright Secured.

Til Kingdom Come

Words & Music by Guy Berryman, Chris Martin, Jon Buckland & Will Champion

THE COLDPLAY COLLECTION

VIVA LA VIDA OR DEATH AND ALL HIS FRIENDS

Life In Technicolor

Words & Music by Guy Berryman, Chris Martin, Jon Buckland, Will Champion & Jon Hopkins

Cemeteries Of London

Words & Music by Guy Berryman, Chris Martin, Jon Buckland & Will Champion

Lost!

Words & Music by Guy Berryman, Chris Martin, Jon Buckland & Will Champion

42

Words & Music by Guy Berryman, Chris Martin, Jon Buckland & Will Champion

Lovers In Japan

Words & Music by Guy Berryman, Chris Martin, Jon Buckland & Will Champion

Reign Of Love

Words & Music by Guy Berryman, Chris Martin, Jon Buckland & Will Champion

Yes

Words & Music by Guy Berryman, Chris Martin, Jon Buckland & Will Champion

Chinese Sleep Chant

Words & Music by Guy Berryman, Chris Martin, Jon Buckland & Will Champion

Viva La Vida

Words & Music by Guy Berryman, Chris Martin, Jon Buckland & Will Champion

Violet Hill

Words & Music by Guy Berryman, Chris Martin, Jon Buckland & Will Champion

Strawberry Swing

Words & Music by Guy Berryman, Chris Martin, Jon Buckland & Will Champion

© Copyright 2008 Universal Music Publishing MGB Limited.
All Rights in Germany Administered by Musik Edition Discoton GmbH (A Division of Universal Music Publishing Group).
All Rights Reserved. International Copyright Secured.

Death And All His Friends

Words & Music by Guy Berryman, Chris Martin, Jon Buckland & Will Champion

The Escapist

Words & Music by Guy Berryman, Chris Martin, Jon Buckland,
Will Champion & Jon Hopkins